An Apple Festival
Orchards in Autumn

Lisa Gabbert

The Rosen Publishing Group's
PowerKids Press ™
New York

For Oma and Opa.

Published in 1999 by The Rosen Publishing Group, Inc.
29 East 21st Street, New York, NY 10010

First Edition

Book Design: Michael de Guzman

Photo Credits: p. 4 © Richard H. Johnston/FPG International; p. 7 © State of Ohio Department of Industrial and Economic Development/FPG International; p. 11 © Dick Luria/FPG International; p. 12 © Edgar Webber/FPG International; p. 15 © Richard Laird/FPG International; p. 16 © Scott Barrow/International Stock; p. 19 © Buddy Mays/FPG International; p. 20 © Phyllis Picardi/International Stock.

Gabbert, Lisa.
    An apple festival: orchards in autumn / by Lisa Gabbert.
        p.   cm. — (Festivals! USA)
    Includes index.
    Summary: Describes the origin and history of apple festivals, an autumn harvest celebration, and tells what goes on there.
    ISBN 0-8239-5342-4
    1. Harvest festivals—United States—Juvenile literature. 2. Apples—United States—Juvenile literature. [1. Harvest festivals. 2. Festivals. 3. Apples.] I. Title. II. Series: Gabbert, Lisa. Festivals! USA.
GT4403.A2G33   1998
394.26—dc21   98-24016
                                             CIP
                                           AC

Manufactured in the United States of America

Contents

An Old Fruit

The apple is a very old fruit that first appeared in Asia. People ate apples during a period of time called the Stone Age. Then the Romans in Italy brought apples to northern Europe. The Europeans carried apple seeds with them when they came to America. Early Dutch and English settlers planted apple **orchards** (OR-cherdz) in their new home. When the **pioneers** (PY-uh-neerz) traveled west, they carried apple seeds and apple trees with them. Apples have always been part of American history.

◀ *Apples are in the same fruit family as peaches, pears, plums, and cherries.*

Johnny Appleseed

Many people know the **legend** (LEH-jend) of Johnny Appleseed. Some versions describe Johnny as a wanderer who wore his cooking pot as a hat. In fact, he was a man named John Chapman, who was born in 1774. He lived along the Pennsylvania and Ohio **frontier** (fron-TEER) and collected apple seeds from **cider mills** (SY-der MILZ) in Pennsylvania. Then he planted the seeds and sold the young trees. Johnny Appleseed was well known and traveled around the country, caring for apple trees.

Johnny Appleseed is part of American history. He is honored around the country with monuments such as this one. ▶

IN MEMORY OF
JOHN
CHAPMAN
BEST KNOWN AS
'JOHNNY
APPLESEED'
PIONEER APPLE
NURSERYMAN OF
RICHLAND COUNTY
FROM 1810 TO 1830

Apple Regions

The United States produces more apples than any other country in the world. Apple trees **blossom** (BLAH-sum) in late spring, when the fruit and flowers of trees can't be harmed by frost. Washington, Michigan, and New York grow most of the apples in the U.S. But apple festivals are held in many states across the country, including Virginia, Pennsylvania, and New York.

◀ *On this map, the states shaded in brown are regions where apples are grown.*

A Harvest Festival

Apple festivals are harvest festivals. They happen when the apple crops are being picked, sometime between late August and mid-October. There are lots of things to eat at apple festivals. There are apple pies, apple turnovers, apple butter, apple pancakes, and apple crisps. Larger festivals have parades, dances, music, and an apple-queen contest. Since apples are grown in the country, most apple festivals are held in small towns rather than large cities.

Apple picking in an orchard is a part of many apple festivals. ▶

10

Cider Mills

Cider mills and apple orchards often hold their own small apple festivals. Some cider mills are old **colonial** (kuh-LOH-nee-ul) houses with apple orchards, hiking trails, and picnic benches on the grounds.

In order to make cider or juice, whole apples are mashed in a **cider press** (SY-der PRESS). Festivals often have old-fashioned wooden cider presses on **display** (dis-PLAY) to show visitors how cider was once made. Some people still make small amounts of cider or juice using hand presses.

Apple orchards are always filled with hundreds of apple trees.

13

Apple Cider and Apple Juice

Sweet apple cider and apple juice are both made by pressing fresh apples. Apple juice is filtered and **pasteurized** (PASS-cher-eyezd) by heating it up to 170 degrees. This kills **bacteria** (bak-TEER-ee-uh). In the past, sweet apple cider was not pasteurized or filtered. It was available only around harvesttime, since it spoiled quickly.

Today many sweet apple ciders are pasteurized and filtered. It can be hard to tell the difference between juice and cider!

Thanks to pasteurization, apple cider and apple juice are available year-round. ▶

Apple Picking

Apple picking is another **tradition** (truh-DIH-shun) that is followed during apple festival time. Some festivals hold tours of the apple orchards and allow visitors to pick their own apples right from the trees. Smart apple pickers twist the stem of the fruit away from the tree as they pull the fruit off the tree. This way a new bud will grow in the same place the following year.

◀ *Apples are still picked by hand, as in colonial times, rather than by a machine.*

Crafts

You can also buy crafts at apple festivals. Crafts are items made by hand. Many festivals sell such crafts as pressed flowers, quilts, baskets, and homemade jams or jellies. One popular activity is making old-fashioned toys, such as shrunken apple head dolls. To make one, a face is carved into an apple. Then the apple is **dehydrated** (dee-HY-dray-ted). The apple shrivels up and is used for the doll's head. The finished doll looks like a funny old man or woman with many wrinkles.

You can find many different kinds of crafts at apple festivals. ▶

Bobbing for Apples

Apple bobbing contests are another part of apple festivals. To play the game, a big tub is filled with water. Apples are dropped in the tub. The apples will float in the water. A player must catch an apple in his or her mouth. This can be difficult, because the apples will often float away. And you can't touch the apples with your hands! Sometimes the winner must dunk his or her head into the tub and push the apple to the bottom in order to catch it.

Bobbing for apples is a very old game that has been around for many years.

Apple Proverbs

Apples are often part of **proverbs** (PRAH-verbs). Has anyone ever said that you are the "apple of my eye" or told you that "An apple a day keeps the doctor away"? Another proverb is "One bad apple spoils the barrel." What do you think these mean?

At apple festivals, you can enjoy apple treats and celebrate a part of American history. Perhaps you and your family can visit one soon!

There may be an apple festival happening near you!

Applefest	Warwick, NY
Apple Cider Days	Stoney Creek Nature Center, Romeo, MI

Glossary

bacteria (bak-TEER-ee-uh) Tiny living things that sometimes cause illness or decay.

blossom (BLAH-sum) A flower from a plant that produces fruit.

cider mill (SY-der MIL) A building where cider is made.

cider press (SY-der PRESS) A machine that mashes apples to make cider or juice.

colonial (kuh-LOH-nee-ul) Having to do with a period of time when the United States was made up of thirteen colonies.

dehydrate (dee-HY-drayt) To take the water out of something.

display (dis-PLAY) To show.

frontier (fron-TEER) An area of the United States that made up the border between settled and unsettled regions.

legend (LEH-jend) A story from the past that many people believe.

orchard (OR-cherd) An area where fruit trees are grown.

pasteurize (PASS-cher-eyez) Heating a liquid to a certain temperature to destroy bacteria.

pioneer (PY-uh-neer) One of the first people to settle in a new area.

proverb (PRAH-verb) A short, well-known saying.

tradition (truh-DIH-shun) Something that has been passed down from parent to child.

Index

TRIBES of NATIVE AMERICA

Lakota

edited by Marla Felkins Ryan
and Linda Schmittroth

BLACKBIRCH®
PRESS

THOMSON
★
™
GALE

San Diego • Detroit • New York • San Francisco • Cleveland
New Haven, Conn. • Waterville, Maine • London • Munich

LIBRARY OF CONGRESS CATALOGING-IN-PUBLICATION DATA

Lakota / Marla Felkins Ryan, book editor; Linda Schmittroth, book editor.
    v. cm. — (Tribes of Native America)
Includes bibliographical references and index.
Contents: Name — A bad start with Americans — Massacre at Wounded Knee — Religion — Daily life — Customs.
  ISBN 1-56711-618-3 (hardback : alk. paper)
  1. Lakota Indians—Juvenile literature. [1. Lakota Indians. 2. Indians of North America—Great Plains.] I. Ryan, Marla Felkins. II. Schmittroth, Linda. III. Series.
  E99.D1 S6172 2003
  978.004'9752—dc21   2002007857

Table of Contents

LAKOTA

Name

The name Lakota *(lah-KOH-tah)* means "allies." The Lakota are also known as Teton Sioux.

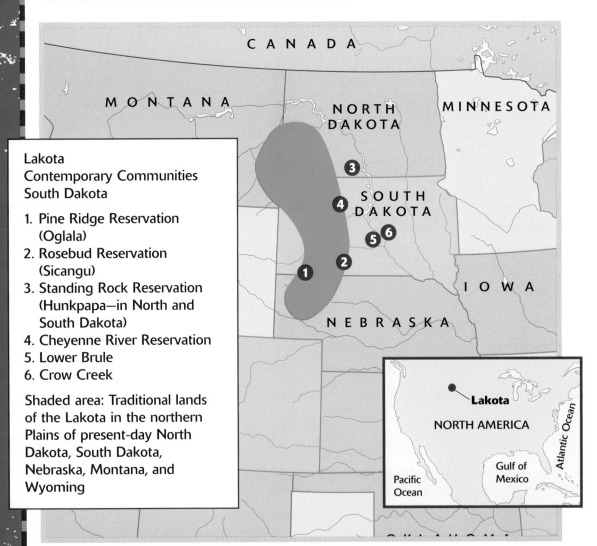

Lakota
Contemporary Communities
South Dakota

1. Pine Ridge Reservation (Oglala)
2. Rosebud Reservation (Sicangu)
3. Standing Rock Reservation (Hunkpapa—in North and South Dakota)
4. Cheyenne River Reservation
5. Lower Brule
6. Crow Creek

Shaded area: Traditional lands of the Lakota in the northern Plains of present-day North Dakota, South Dakota, Nebraska, Montana, and Wyoming

CANADA

MONTANA

NORTH DAKOTA

MINNESOTA

SOUTH DAKOTA

NEBRASKA

IOWA

Lakota

NORTH AMERICA

Pacific Ocean

Gulf of Mexico

Atlantic Ocean

Where are the traditional Lakota lands?

In the mid-1700s, the Lakota moved from Minnesota to the Black Hills of western South Dakota, eastern Wyoming, and eastern Montana. Today, they live on reservations in North and South Dakota. Some also live at Fort Peck Reservation in Montana.

The Lakota moved to the Black Hills of South Dakota (pictured) in the mid-1700s.

What has happened to the population?

In a 1990 population count by the U.S. Bureau of the Census, more than 91,000 people identified themselves as part of a Sioux tribe.

Origins and group ties

Some legends trace the tribe's origins to the Black Hills. Other stories say the tribe came from the Minnesota woodlands, where they and the Nakota were part of the Dakota tribe. In the mid-1700s, the Dakota tribe broke into three groups. The Dakota stayed in Minnesota. The other two groups, which were called Lakota and Nakota, moved to the West.

A Lakota father and daughter. The Lakota was once the most powerful tribe in America.

The Pine Ridge Reservation in South Dakota. The Dakota broke into three groups in the mid-1700s.

The Lakota was once the most powerful tribe in North America and controlled a large area of the northern Great Plains. Lakota leaders—including Sitting Bull, Crazy Horse, and Red Cloud—were among the best-known Native Americans of the 19th century. In recent times, the Lakota have been at the forefront of the Indian rights movement.

Red Cloud was one of the best-known Native Americans of the 19th century.

HISTORY

Golden Age of the Lakota people

When they moved to the Great Plains, the Lakota came to depend on buffalo. From these animals, the Lakota got food, clothing, shelter, weapons, and household objects. They followed the great herds as they migrated.

During the late 18th century, the Lakota split into 7 bands. When they joined with the Northern Cheyenne and Northern Arapaho tribes, the Lakota became a strong force. The years from 1775 to 1868 are sometimes called the tribe's Golden Age.

Meriwether Lewis and William Clark talk with Native Americans. The Lakota first met whites when Lewis and Clark passed through their territory in 1804.

A bad start with Americans

The Lakota first met white Americans in 1804, when the Lewis and Clark expedition passed through their lands. The first meeting went badly, with misunderstandings on both sides.

The second meeting started off better. Lewis and Clark were allowed to watch a scalp dance, the first ever seen by Americans. When the Lakota disliked the gifts Lewis and Clark gave them, though, the meeting went sour. Lewis wrote that he found the Sioux to be "the vilest miscreants [evildoers] of the savage race."

Lewis and Clark's visit was a warning that the United States would claim Sioux lands. In 1825, the government sent soldiers to sign treaties with the Indians.

Treaty era begins

In 1825, treaties were signed with three Lakota bands. The United States claimed the right to control trade in the region. It also agreed not to let whites trespass on Lakota land.

The Lakota liked to trade with Americans for goods such as guns and cooking utensils, but the whites also brought diseases. As the Lakota became dependent on American goods, they also suffered disease epidemics.

1869
The Transcontinental Railroad is completed

1874
Gold is found in the Black Hills

1876
Lakota warriors defeat Lieutenant Colonel George Armstrong Custer in the Battle of the Little Bighorn

1890
Sitting Bull is murdered. U.S. troops kill more than 300 Lakota men, women, and children in the Massacre at Wounded Knee

1973
American Indian Movement (AIM) activists occupy Wounded Knee and engage in a 71-day standoff with government agents

1980
Lakota refuse a $105 million payment for the wrongful taking of their territory

The inside of Fort Laramie. The Lakota signed the Fort Laramie Treaty in 1851.

Wagon trains head west

Until the 1840s, relations between whites and Indians on the Great Plains were fairly peaceful. Then, wagon trains headed west. As white settlers crossed Lakota lands, they drove away the buffalo. To stop white pioneers, the tribe threatened, robbed, and attacked wagon trains. Nothing worked.

In 1850, the western tribes learned that the U.S. government wished to talk peace at Fort Laramie, Wyoming. Thousands of Indians went to the fort.

Fort Laramie Treaty made and broken

The Lakota signed the Fort Laramie Treaty of 1851. It gave them rights to more than 60 million acres of land, including the Black Hills. The Lakota agreed to let settlers pass safely on the Oregon Trail.

THE SEVEN LAKOTA BANDS

Shortly after they settled in the Black Hills, the Lakota split into seven bands:

Oglala (which means "They Scatter Their Own"), the largest group, occupied western South Dakota, southeastern Montana, and northeastern Wyoming.

Sicangu or Brulé ("Burned Thighs"), lived in northern Nebraska and southern South Dakota.

Miniconjou ("Planters by the Water"), occupied central and northern South Dakota.

Oohenonpa ("Two Kettles"), occupied land just west of the Missouri River in South Dakota.

Hunkpapa ("End of the Entrance"), **Itazipco** or **Sans Arcs** ("Without Bows"), and **Sihasapa** ("Black Feet") lived on lands farther north.

Hunters in the Oglala band. The Oglala band was the largest group in the Lakota tribe.

The treaty did not last long. Violence erupted as tribes fought over trade and hunting grounds. Meanwhile, the U.S. Senate changed the treaty. The treaty had promised annual payments to the Indians for 50 years. The Senate decided it would pay for only 10 years.

In 1857, thousands of Sioux vowed not to let whites take any more of their land. Then, in 1859, gold was found in Colorado. Gold was later found in Montana as well, and more whites traveled westward. Many decided to stay and explore the Lakota hunting grounds. It seemed that it would take war to end the land disputes.

Red Cloud's War

The Sioux wars began in Minnesota in 1862. American army soldiers had orders to kill every

Several Native American tribes signed the Fort Laramie Treaty of 1868. The Lakota received half of South Dakota from the U.S. government.

male Indian over age 12. Women and children were not spared, either.

In 1865, after the American Civil War, Congress focused on Indian issues. Some starving Lakota groups signed treaties. Thousands of others, led by Red Cloud (1822–1909), remained hostile. When the Americans said they wanted peace, but also intended to build forts and roads, Red Cloud declared: "I am for war."

Red Cloud's War lasted from 1866 to 1868. Crazy Horse and other Lakota warriors led successful attacks against soldiers in American forts. The government admitted defeat in 1868. In the Fort Laramie Treaty of 1868, the Lakota won the Great Sioux Reservation, which made up half of what is now South Dakota. The Indians were also awarded the Bighorn Mountain region of Wyoming and Nebraska. They were given tools, cattle, and other materials to help them become farmers and ranchers.

Gold was found in the Black Hills in 1874. The U.S. government tried to buy the Black Hills from the Lakota. The tribe refused because they considered the land sacred. The U.S. Army was sent in 1876 to force the Lakota to give up their traditional lifestyle and land. Intense fighting followed in the War for the Black Hills. This war was also called Sitting Bull and Crazy Horse's War.

Chief Crazy Horse led successful attacks against U.S. soldiers in the Battle of the Little Bighorn.

Sitting Bull and Crazy Horse's War

In 1876, the Lakota won several major battles. At the Battle of the Little Bighorn, Lakota fighters led by Crazy Horse, Sitting Bull, and another leader named Gall defeated and killed famed army commander George Armstrong Custer and all his men.

This battle was the last great Indian victory. Over the next six months, the Lakota suffered many defeats. By mid-1877, many Lakota chiefs had surrendered and gone to reservations.

Lakota war chief Gall helped defeat George Armstrong Custer at the Battle of the Little Bighorn.

Native Americans re-enact the Battle of the Little Bighorn. This was the last big victory for Native American warriors.

Sitting Bull (center) with his mother (left) and daughter. Sitting Bull moved to Canada to escape the U.S. Army in the late 1800s.

In September 1877, the U.S. Army tried to put Crazy Horse in prison. He was killed when he resisted arrest. Sitting Bull and his followers fled to safety in Canada.

Lakota resistance broken

On January 31, 1876, Congress said that the Black Hills belonged to the United States. The Lakota were ordered to move.

South Dakota became a state in 1889. The Sioux Act of 1889 broke the Great Sioux Reservation into four smaller reservations. Individual Sioux were given plots of land. The land left over was made available to white settlers.

Massacre at Wounded Knee

This painting shows the capture and death of Sitting Bull at Standing Rock Reservation.

In 1881, Sitting Bull and his people surrendered to the U.S. Army. Eventually, he went to live on the Standing Rock Reservation. In 1890, the U.S. government began to fear that Sitting Bull might again lead Indians against white settlers. Tribal police were sent to arrest him. A fight broke out, and the chief was killed by the police.

AMERICAN INDIAN MOVEMENT

In 1968, a Yankton-Oglala Sioux named Russell Means, together with Dennis Banks, Clyde Bellecourt, and other Native Americans, founded the American Indian Movement (AIM). In 1972, AIM sponsored an event called the Trail of Broken Treaties. A large group of people walked from Seattle, Washington, to Washington, D.C., to protest the treatment of Indians by the government.

In 1973, AIM activists held a protest at the town of Wounded Knee, near the site of the Wounded Knee Massacre. Surrounded by federal agents, the armed group occupied the site for 71 days. During this time, two AIM members were killed. Thirty activists were arrested at the end of the standoff. All were set free because of illegal actions by the government.

In 1975, two FBI agents were killed in a shootout with AIM activists on the Pine Ridge Reservation. AIM member Leonard Peltier and two other Lakota men were charged with

Russell Means helped found the American Indian Movement (AIM) in 1968.

murder. Peltier was found guilty and sentenced to life in prison. The others were found not guilty. Since then, information has suggested that the government used underhanded tricks to make sure Peltier was found guilty. Many people and groups have asked for a new trial for Peltier, but this has not yet happened.

AIM activists staged a protest in the town of Wounded Knee in 1973.

Next, troops were sent to arrest Lakota leader Big Foot. He and his followers were headed to Pine Ridge Reservation, where he hoped to make peace. He was stopped and ordered to set up camp near Wounded Knee Creek. When the soldiers tried to disarm his men, a rifle went off. A battle followed, in which more than 300 Sioux were killed. Many of them were women and children. This incident was called the Massacre at Wounded Knee.

Reservation years

The tribe continued to lose land through the early 1900s as the reservations were broken into small plots. The Lakota also lost parts of their culture. Their children were sent to boarding schools, and

missionaries came to convert the Lakota to Christianity. For many years, traditional ceremonies and practices were not allowed.

Carlisle Indian School in Pennsylvania. In the 1900s, many Lakota children were sent to boarding schools.

The Lakota's modern challenges

In the 20th century, the Lakota's main struggle was to regain lost land. That battle continues today. The Lakota have never accepted the United States's 1877 claim to the Black Hills. They believe that these lands were given to them in the Fort Laramie Treaty of 1868.

In 1980, the U.S. Supreme Court awarded the Lakota $105 million for the loss of their lands a century earlier. The Lakota refused the settlement. They did not want money—they wanted their lands returned to them.

Religion

Sioux Indians perform the Ghost Dance. This dance was a type of peaceful rebellion.

The Lakota believe that all living things are linked. Their god, known as Wakan Tanka, or the Great Mystery Power or Creator, includes all elements of nature.

In 1890, the Lakota reacted to their loss of freedom by practicing the Ghost Dance Religion. The tribe had lost most of its basic ways of life and faced terrible conditions. The Ghost Dance was a form of peaceful resistance. The U.S. government eventually outlawed the ceremony, but the Lakota continued to perform it.

Government

The Lakota traditionally lived in small settlements that had no powerful leaders. In the 1800s, they began to unite in larger groups who supported strong leaders. Once the Lakota were on reservations, government agents discouraged the system of having head chiefs.

This painted buffalo hide depicts stories of a buffalo hunt. After the Sioux acquired horses, they depended on the trade of buffalo hides.

The Indian Reorganization Act of 1934 called for elected tribal councils at several reservations. Some traditional Lakota leaders have called the tribal councils corrupt. Many believe the councils do not fairly represent their people.

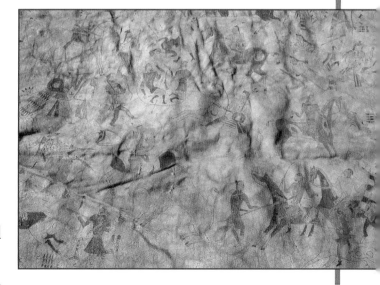

Economy

Before they moved to the Great Plains, the Sioux tribes hunted, fished, gathered, and farmed. After they moved

The Pine Ridge Indian Reservation in South Dakota. The Lakota reservations were some of the poorest in the 1990s.

and acquired horses, the economy came to depend on the trade of buffalo hides. The Lakota raided other tribes for horses, and drove many of the tribes away. This helped them dominate the Great Plains trade.

After the first treaties were signed with the U.S. government, many Lakota people had to take government handouts to survive because most of the buffalo were gone. On the other hand, many became farmers and ranchers. They were successful until the Great Depression—a severe economic downturn—struck in the 1930s. Many Lakota had to lease their lands to white farmers.

Lakota reservations were some of the poorest communities in the United States in the 1990s. Casinos, bingo halls, and small businesses have been started to expand the economy.

DAILY LIFE

Education

In the 1880s, Red Cloud asked the U.S. government to let priests come to reservations to start schools. Many Sioux children went to these schools.

Today, reservation schools teach Lakota language and culture. Traditional education begins with Head Start programs for preschoolers and continues through college.

Sitting Bull's family in front of their tepee. The Lakota lived in tepees as did many other tribes who lived on the Great Plains.

Buildings

Like many tribes of the Great Plains, the Lakota lived in tepees. A framework of wooden poles was set up in a cone shape. The poles were covered with buffalo skins that were carefully prepared and stitched together. After about 1900, Lakota tepees were replaced by tents and then by log cabins.

Lakota men hunted elk (pictured), buffalo, and deer.

Food

The great buffalo herds provided most of the food for the Lakota. Their diet consisted almost entirely of buffalo and chokecherries.

Lakota men did most of the hunting. Women butchered the animals, prepared the hides, and cooked or preserved the meat. Besides buffalo, the Lakota also hunted deer, elk, and small game. They gathered roots and berries, and traded for food with other tribes.

Clothing

Lakota men wore fringed buckskin shirts and leggings, often decorated with brightly colored porcupine quills or locks of hair. They also wore buckskin moccasins with tough buffalo-hide soles. They adorned themselves with earrings, armbands, and bear-claw necklaces. Younger men often shaved the sides of their heads and let the hair in the middle grow long.

Women wore buckskin dresses that reached to the ankle over leggings that went to the knee. Their clothing, too, was elaborately decorated with fringes, porcupine quills, or beads. The women usually let their hair grow long and wore it in two braids woven with pieces of cloth or beads.

Lakota children, both girls and boys, had their ears pierced when they were five or six. From then on, they wore strings of colored beads as earrings.

Lakota men wore fringed and decorated buckskin shirts.

Lakota women wore decorated buckskin dresses over leggings.

Healing practices

Lakota healers handled illnesses and injuries. Healers made medicine out of herbs, tree bark, wild fruits, and ground buffalo hooves. They also asked spirits to help diagnose and cure illnesses through song, dance, and special prayers.

Oral literature

Some Sioux origin stories say that the Dakota, Lakota, and Nakota peoples first came from the Black Hills. According to their oral traditions, the Sioux first lived beneath the earth's surface. Later, they emerged through Wind Cave, but left their leader behind. Their leader then came above the surface as a buffalo, and offered his body to be used for everything the people needed to survive.

CUSTOMS

War and hunting rituals

Anyone who could convince a group of volunteers to follow him into battle could be a war chief. After a successful battle, the Lakota held scalp dances to celebrate. During the annual wani-sapa, or "fall hunt," hundreds of Lakota worked in large groups to hunt enough game to supply the tribe with food for the winter.

Vision quests

Around the time they reached puberty, all Lakota men (and some women) traditionally took part in a vision quest. The purpose of the vision quest was to

A Native American praying. When they reached puberty, Lakota men took part in a vision quest.

make a personal connection with the supernatural being who would guide them through life. First, the young person was purified in a sweat lodge. Then two helpers built a platform at a sacred place, and left the vision seeker alone there. The vision seeker paced on the platform, prayed, smoked a sacred pipe, and fasted. He or she kept track of everything he or she saw and heard during this time.

After four days, the helpers returned and brought the seeker back to camp. There, the spiritual leaders explained his or her vision. After a successful vision quest, a Lakota was considered an adult in the tribe.

Courtship and marriage

Marriages were usually arranged by a young couple's parents. Sometimes, however, couples fell in love and decided to elope. The couple was formally recognized as husband and wife when the two families gave gifts and the couple moved into a tepee together.

Death and burial

When a member of the Lakota tribe died, his or her body was placed on a raised platform or in the branches of a tree. Some possessions and food for the journey to the next world were placed with the body. Though the Lakota were expected to face their own death with dignity, they mourned the loss of relatives deeply.

Current tribal issues

The Lakota continue to fight for the return of their traditional lands rather than accept a cash settlement. The people are also divided between those who wish to keep the old Lakota ways and those who prefer to accept mainstream American culture.

Chief Arvol Looking Horse gives a speech at the United Nations in New York City. The Lakota continue to fight for their traditional lands.

Olympic runner Billy Mills set a world record at the 1964 Olympics.

Notable people

Sitting Bull (c.1834–1890) was a great chief of the Hunkpapa band of Lakota. A medicine man, he inspired the Lakota warriors who defeated Custer at the Battle of the Little Bighorn in 1876. The next year, he was forced to flee to Canada. He surrendered to the United States in 1881 and went to live on a reservation. Tribal police killed him on December 15, 1890.

Billy Mills (1938–) set a world record in track at the 1964 Olympic Games. He then returned to Pine Ridge Reservation as a role model for young people. Today, he is a spokesperson for Indian causes.

Red Cloud (1822–1909) was a tribal leader and warrior. He was known for his resistance to the occupation of the Dakota land by American settlers. He later tried to make peace between his people and the U.S. government.

Mary Brave Bird (also known as Mary Crow Dog, 1953–) dictated two books about the American Indian Movement.

Russell Means (1939–), Indian rights activist, helped to found the American Indian Movement (AIM).

Ben Reifel (1906–1990) was the first member of the Sioux Nation to serve in the U.S. Congress.

For more information

Ambrose, Stephen. "Encounter with the Sioux" in *Undaunted Courage: Meriwether Lewis, Thomas Jefferson, and the Opening of the American West.* New York: Simon & Schuster, 1996.

"The Battle of Little Bighorn." An eyewitness account by the Lakota Chief Red Horse recorded in pictographs and text at the Cheyenne River Reservation, 1881. http://www.pbs.org/weta/hewest/wpages/wpgs660/bighorn.htm.

Bonvillain, Nancy. *The Teton Sioux.* New York: Chelsea House, 1994.

Brown, Dee. *Bury My Heart at Wounded Knee: An Indian History of the American West.* New York: Holt, Rinehart, and Winston, 1970.

Cheyenne River Sioux Tribe web site. http://www.sioux.org

Dolan, Terrance. *The Teton Sioux Indians.* New York: Chelsea House, 1995.

Freedman, Russell. *The Life and Death of Crazy Horse.* New York: Holiday House, 1996.

A Guide to the Great Sioux Nation. http://www.state.sd.us/state/executive/tourism/sioux/sioux.htm.

Larson, Robert W. *Red Cloud: Warrior-Statesman of the Lakota Sioux.* Norman: University of Oklahoma Press, 1997.

Lazarus, Edward. *Black Hills White Justice: The Sioux Nation Versus the United States, 1775 to the Present.* New York: HarperCollins, 1991.

Rosebud Reservation home page. http://www.littlesioux.org

Timeline of events relevant to the Northern Plains tribes. http://www.hanksville.phast.umass.edu/june95/lakota/timeline2.html.

Glossary

Native original inhabitant

Rebellion an often violent uprising

Reservation land set aside and given to Native Americans

Ritual something that is custom or done in a certain way

Sacred highly valued and important

Tradition a custom or an established pattern of behavior

Treaty agreement

Tribe a group of people who live together in a community

Index